JANUSZ PODLECKI
WIELICZKA
HISTORIC SALT MINE

THE WIELICZKA SALT MINE WAS ENTERED
IN THE FIRST UNESCO WORLD HERITAGE LIST IN 1978

The salt mines of Wieliczka are no less magnificent than the Egyptian pyramids,
but more useful. They are an illustrious reminder of the industry of the Poles...
Le Laboureur, 1647

'WIELICZKA' SALT MINE

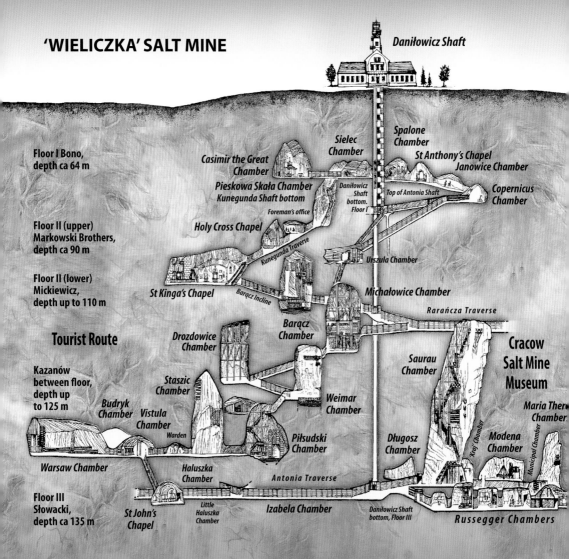

Daniłowicz Shaft

Floor I Bono,
depth ca 64 m

Casimir the Great Chamber

Sielec Chamber

Spalone Chamber

St Anthony's Chapel

Janowice Chamber

Pieskowa Skała Chamber

Kunegunda Shaft bottom

Daniłowicz Shaft bottom. Floor I

Top of Antonia Shaft

Copernicus Chamber

Foreman's office

Holy Cross Chapel

Floor II (upper)
Markowski Brothers,
depth ca 90 m

Kunegunda Traverse

Urszula Chamber

Floor II (lower)
Mickiewicz,
depth up to 110 m

St Kinga's Chapel

Barącz Incline

Michałowice Chamber

Rarańcza Traverse

Barącz Chamber

Tourist Route

Drozdowice Chamber

Saurau Chamber

Cracow
Salt Mine
Museum

Kazanów
between floor,
depth up
to 125 m

Staszic Chamber

Weimar Chamber

Maria There Chamber

Budryk Chamber

Vistula Chamber

Warden

Piłsudski Chamber

Długosz Chamber

Modena Chamber

Kraj Chamber

Municipal Chamber

Warsaw Chamber

Haluszka Chamber

Antonia Traverse

Floor III
Słowacki,
depth ca 135 m

St John's Chapel

Little Haluszka Chamber

Izabela Chamber

Daniłowicz Shaft bottom, Floor III

Russegger Chambers

VISIT THE TOURIST ROUTE IN THE WIELICZKA SALT MINE

Period	April 1 – Oct. 31	Nov. 2 – March 31	Holy Saturday	Dec. 31
Visiting hours	7.30 a.m. – 7.30 p.m.	8.00 a.m. – 5.00 p.m.	7.30 a.m. – 1.45 p.m.	8.00 a.m. – 2.00 p.m.
Route closed	Jan. 1, Nov. 1, Dec. 24–25, Easter Sunday			

The ticket includes a visit to the underground exhibition
of the Cracow Salt Mine Museum.

KOPALNIA SOLI „WIELICZKA" – TRASA TURYSTYCZNA Sp. z o.o.
32-020 Wieliczka, ul. Daniłowicza 10 – DZIAŁ ORGANIZACJI TURYSTYKI
Tel. (+48) 12 278-73-02, (+48) 12 278-73-66. Fax (+48) 12 278-73-33
www.kopalnia.pl   e-mail: turystyka@kopalnia.pl

'WIELICZKA' SALT MINE – TOURIST ROUTE LTD.

JANUSZ PODLECKI

WIELICZKA
HISTORIC SALT MINE

Introduction
STANISŁAW ANIOŁ

Fourth edition

PUBLISHING HOUSE 'KARPATY' – ANDRZEJ ŁĄCZYŃSKI
CRACOW 2012

1. Settlement in the Wieliczka area connected with saltworks started already in the Neolithic period (ca 4500-1700 B.C. The maquette in the Sielec Caamber which shows a Neolithic saltworks and the villages of early settlers (left) was made on the basis of experimental research by Professor Paweł Valde-Nowak of the Polish Academy of Arts and sciences.

The traditional miners' blessing greets everybody who wishes to visit the subterranean labyrinth of the Wieliczka Salt Mine. The unique character and beauty of the mine was created by nature about fifteen million years ago. The Wieliczka salt deposit was formed after the waters of a Miocene sea had evaporated, and its interesting geological structure is the result of the later uplift of the Carpathian Mountains: it is the block type in the upper stratum and the stratified type in the lower one. Although the tradition of obtaining salt from brine in the vicinity of Wieliczka goes back about 5,000 years, that is to the Neolithic period, the archaeological evidence concerning settlement in the area does not suggest that the local population grew rich before the eleventh century. A significant development of Wieliczka took place between the eleventh and the thirteenth centuries, which is corroborated by the charter granted to the settlement in 1289 by the Duke of Silesia and Cracow, Henry IV Probus. The Franconian law charter was confirmed and extended by Duke Przemysł II in 1290.

Obtaining salt from brine must have been fairly developed as the brine well discovered near the present Daniłowicza Street is dated to the twelfth century. Surface salt springs must have become exhausted, which led to constructing wells and drawing up brine. This way of exploiting salt waters seems to have led to the discovery of rock-salt. The oldest known and located Goryszowski shaft, where rock-salt was mined, was built in the second half of the thirteenth century. The continuous struggle of man with the nature of the Wieliczka deposit has been going on ever since.

The Wieliczka Mine reflects the achievement of simple miners and engineers, of Polish kings and of eminent scientists, which took from the Middle Ages; it portrays the development of technology and labour, as well as the history of the micro-society which evolved around the mining establishment.

Obtaining and sale of salt in the Wieliczka Mine was always the right of the ruler, who entrusted it to his loyal men or leased it out. The proceeds from salt under the Piast and Jagiellon kings provided almost 1/3 of the royal revenue. In 1368 King Casimir the Great codified the customary law of the country, which meant that the rights of the miners of Wieliczka and Bochnia who worked 'grey gold' became regulated by statute.

The miners at Wieliczka slowly but steadily came to know the mine and discovered its secrets and abundance. The caverns left by mining salt were given timber supports, and the

2. Brine springs which gradually dried up were deepened to obtain brine, and thus brine wells appeared. Most probably, while deepening wells, some lumps of rock-salt were found. The oldest known and located Goryszowski shaft, where rock-salt was mined, was built in the second half of the 13th c. The Daniłowicz Shaft (right) was sunk in the first half of the 17th c, and now serves tourist traffic.

water which flew into the mine was treated to produce salt. In the nine centuries of mining in Wieliczka, about 7.5 million cubic metres of salt were extracted, which is equivalent to a train measuring about 1/5 of the length of the equator.

The Wieliczka Mine has nine working floors: from the first one, at 64 metres underground, to the last one, at the depth of 327 metres. The total length of galleries is about 250 kilometres. The chambers hollowed by generations of miners in the course of several centuries amount to 2040 workings. We can apprehend the huge size of the mine when having walked along the tourist route we realise that it contains only 3 per cent of all workings.

Stubbornly but humbly, the miners quarried salt, constructed drawing machines, and harnessed horses to transport yielded salt. Huge blocks of salt were hollowed from inside so that a layer of intact rock-salt was left, which for centuries withstood the pressure of the rock mass. The works on one such block often lasted for several generations of miners.

The salt labyrinth of Wieliczka was well known in medieval Europe. Still, each descent into the mine was hazardous: work there was very dangerous, many miners were killed, and many more suffered injuries.

Their dangerous work made the miners more religious than other social groups. The custom has survived of erecting a cross at the spot where a miner perished. Chapels were constructed underground and services said. When in 1697 a chapel was consumed by fire, a royal commission forbade to furnish chapels with inflammable items. Paradoxically, this prohibition resulted in developing the unique tradition of rock-salt sculpture which has been kept up in the mine for over three centuries. Rock-salt sculptures were carved by miners. The greatest achievement of the self-taught sculptors is the admirable and graceful chapel of St Kinga (1896), carved 101 metres underground.

According to the legend, St Kinga, daughter of King Bela IV of Hungary, was responsible for discovering the rock-salt deposit at Wieliczka. On her marriage to the Polish Duke Bolesław the Chaste, she received a salt mine at Marmaros as her dowry. She cast her engagement ring into the shaft of the mine. When on the way to Cracow Kinga's retinue stopped near Wieliczka, she ordered a well to be dug. Yet instead of water, salt was discovered, and in the first lump of salt extracted, Kinga's engagement ring was found. Thus St Kinga became the patroness of salt miners.

There are a number of chapels on the tourist route in the mine. St Anthony's Chapel on floor I, carved in rock-salt, is seriously damaged but still beautiful. From 1698 mass used to be said there at the beginning of each workday. The Holy Cross Chapel (mid-seventeenth century) which has been moved to floor II from an unsafe place, contains some of the few wooden sculptures in the mine, representing Christ Crucified and Our Lady the Victorious (17th c.). In 2005 the mid-nineteenth-century the beautiful timber St John's Chapel was moved to floor III. Until then it had been on floor I, away from the Tourist Route.

In the feeble flame of the miner's lamp, the mine interior seemed dim and mysterious, and imagination animated and magnified everything. Thus a number of tales and legends about the mine were created. The tales about „Him", or the Warden, who takes care of the miners' safety, are still widely circulated. The Warden has been assigned a chamber on the tourist route in the mine.

The first plans of the Wieliczka Mine were produced by Marcin German in 1638, and decorated with engravings by Wilhelm Hondius in 1645. It is a rich source of information on the mine at the time and on miners' work. We can see there 'the devil's ride', that is miners sliding down a rope. It was the privilege of senior miners, while the younger ones walked down the mine by stairs and ladders. There are also pictures of the drawing machines on the surface which were operated by horses. In the seventeenth century there were about 100 horses working in the mine.

Mining rock-salt was a dangerous job but the miners were further threatened by the elements: fire, water and mine gas. Water leaks – the danger miners have been struggling with – frequently threatened the mine and the town built above it. The most recent flooding of the mine in 1992 resulted in serious damage. At present the mine has been coping with about 200 leaks. Fire was a frightful threat, particularly when open flame was used to lighten the mine; it was very serious as fires in a mine were difficult to quench. One of the largest fires, in 1644, raged in the mine for eight months. Ventilating the mine and the presence of methane, known there as 'saltpetre', were also a major problem. Bellows and pumps were constructed to ventilate the mine, and 'saltpetre' was burnt out by experienced miners who were called 'penitents'. Now the mine is efficiently ventilated by three ventilating systems.

The mine employed the people who lived in the Wieliczka area and were organised in fairly numerous mining brotherhoods. Run by leaseholders, the mine functioned more or less efficiently. The brotherhoods defended the miners' interests, yet rebellions in the mine occurred from time to time. The most serious of them took place in 1690; it was suppressed by soldiers and ended in a trial followed by death sentences or flogging.

The Wieliczka Mine boasts the largest known specimen of Miocene mineralogy: the Crystal Caves. The natural caverns 80 meters under the earth surface display brilliant halite crystals, their longest edges up to 50 centimetres. The caves were discovered in the late nineteenth century and they have lost some of the crystals (the largest set of crystals from the Wieliczka Mine is to be found in Vienna, and weighs almost a ton). Rare visitors are nevertheless spellbound by their beauty. The caves, which are about three kilometres away from the underground tourist route, are strictly protected as the most unique attractions in the mine.

In 1978 the Wieliczka Salt Mine was entered by the UNESCO on the first list of the World Cultural and Natural Heritage, and in 1994 it was recognised, by a decree of the President of Poland, as a Polish historic monument.

Welcome to the mine, and enjoy and appreciate this unique human achievement – the testimony of human spiritual power, courage and industriousness, humility and passion.

UNDERGROUND GALLERIES, CHAMBERS AND LAKES

3. Previous page: wooden drains directed underground water leaks to wooden tubs, and then to tanks at shaft bottom, and then by shaft to the surface.

4-6. The Pieskowa Skała Chamber worked already in the 17th c. century is the only one on the tourist route which was worked by the pickaxe. Salt was carried up in barrels (above) by the simplest hauling device, the hand-operated cross (left).

7, 8. Water was carried to wooden tubs also in wooden jugs. The device known as 'paternoster' (below) used to pump up brine, haul it up to an upper floor and direct it to tanks at shaft bottom.

9, 10. 'Carriers' were miners who carried up salt in bags on their backs or in wooden troughs in their hands, while 'water' miners carried water up in wooden jugs.

11-13. A small lake and timbering emphasise the beauty of the Erazm Barącz Chamber, which was worked in he years 1846-1866, and named after the mine manager in 1917-1918.

14, 15. The Sielec Gallery – in the Wieliczka mine horses worked from the 16th c. They carried salt along galleries or moved the treadmills (hauling devices). Below: the treadmill of the Saxon type (18th c.), in the Casimir the Great Chamber, worked already in the first half of the 18th c.

16, 17. The spray chamber owes its fantastic shape to the miners who quarried salt by washing it out from the deposit. Below: the Stanisław Staszic Chamber, worked in the years 1871-1914, is of the greatest height on the tourist route and reaches up to 36 m (50 m before its lower part was filled up).

18, 19. The Józef Piłsudski Chamber was hollowed in two adjacent blocks of rock-salt in 1810-1830 and is connected by a small lake. The timber basket construction which supports it is admired by visitors.

20. The Gothic timbering of the Michałowice Chamber, worked for almost 100 years from ca 1685, is the product of the o skilled carpentry of the miners. →

21. The Drozdowice Chamber,
hollowed at the turn of the 17th
and 18th c. The monument of
two mine carpenters (1967)
is the work of the miner
sculptor Antoni Wyrodek.

22, 23. The Weimar Chamber,
worked in the early 20th c.
(10,000 cubic meters), with
a lake, like, any chambers in
the mine, commands respect
for the work of the Wieliczka
miners.

24-27. The mine displays the element of earth. The timbering cracks under the pressure of the rock mass and has to be replaced periodically.

28, 29. The micro-climate in the chambers in the Wieliczka mine is used for treatment and rehabilitation of patients. The sanatorium chamber on floor V (211 m underground), named after. Professor Skulimowski, the founder of the allergological sanatorium. Below: the sanatorium in the Wessel Chamber on floor III (135 m underground).

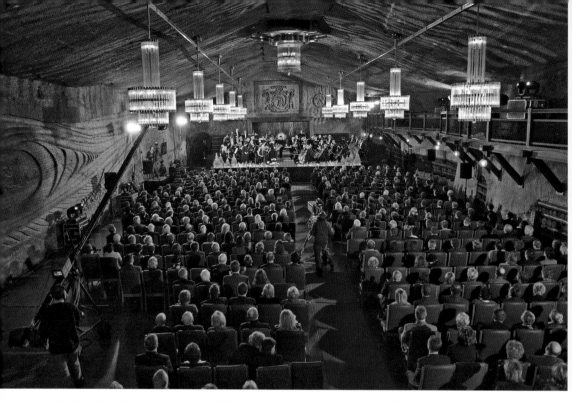

30, 31. The Warsaw Chamber (125 m underground) was worked in the 19th c., and now it is used for cultural and sports events. Below: in the adjacent Budryk Chamber tourists can rest after their underground walk and have a snack.

32. A section of the rock-salt sculpture composition, 'The Great Legend' in the Janowice Chamber. →

THE ART
OF THE MINERS

33-36. St Kinga's Chapel, 101 m underground (previous page) was started in 1896 and is a masterpiece carved in rock-salt by the Wieliczka the miner sculptors: the brothers Józef and Tomasz Markowski, and Antoni Wyrodek. 'Flight into Egypt', 1927-1928 (above) and 'The Miracle at Cana-in Galilee' (1929) are the reliefs carved by Antoni Wyrodek. The high altar (1895-1898) with the statue of St Kinga (1920), (right) is the work of Józef Markowski and his assistants.

37-40. St Kinga's Chapel, the works carved in rock-salt by Józef Markowski: the side altar of the Holy Heart of Jesus, and the Resurrection Chapel, ca 1920, (above) and (below) Christ Crucified (the sculpture won an award at the Paris Exhibition in 1900). Below (left): St Barbara, the patroness of miners, carved in transparent Wieliczka salt.

41, 42. Antoni Wyrodek was the only miner sculptor sent to study art in Cracow. In St Kinga's Chapel, he carved in rock-salt, as a self-taught sculptor the relief 'Twelve Years Old Christ Preaching in the Temple', 1927-1928 (above), and as a professional sculptor, the relief 'Doubting Thomas', 1962-1963 (below).

43, 44. St Kinga's Chapel; rock-salt reliefs 'Herod's Sentence' (above) and 'The Massacre of the Innocents' (below) by Tomasz Markowski (the younger of the brothers), 1920-1927.

45, 46. St Kinga's Chapel; Leonardo da Vinci's fresco 'The Last Supper' was the model for the rock-salt relief (1936-1945) by Antoni Wyrodek. The Bethlehem crib (below) was carved (1903-1920) in wood by Józef Markowski, and the present figures were made by Mieczysław Kluzek in the 1970s.

47-51. St Kinga's Chapel, rock-salt sculptures carved by the Markowski brothers (above): the pulpit (1903), the symbol of the living Polish nation, and the legendary moment of the discovery of the Wieliczka rock-salt deposit (1920-1927). Rock-salt sculptures by Antoni Wyrodek (below): detail from 'Flight into Egypt'(1927--1928) and St Kinga (1930-1935). Right: rock-salt sculpture of the blessed Pope John Paul II (by Stanisław Anioł and his team, 1999), carred to thank for the canonization of the blessed Kinga.

52-54. St Anthony's Chapel, where services at the beginning of each workday were said already in 1698. The sculptures carved in rock-salt by an unknown miner have been partly damaged in the course of time, mainly by moist air.

55-57. The Holy Cross Chapel was created in the mid-19th c. The 17th c. wooden sculptures of Christ Crucified and Our Lady the Victorious were transferred there. Below: the beautiful timber St John' Chapel, where Mass was said already in 1859, has been moved from the Lipowiec Chamber (floor I) to the Tourist Route (floor III).

58, 59. The Spalone Chamber, worked before 1783 – 'Penitents', rock-salt sculptures (1972) carved by the miner Mieczysław Kluzek, represent the miners burning out methane.

60. The Janowice Chamber, worked in the first half of the 17th c., the set of rock-salt sculptures, 'The Great Legend' (1967), the work of the miner Mieczysław Kluzek, shows the moment of the discovery of the ring, which, according to the legend, travelled with salt from Hungary to Poland.

61. The Casimir the Great Chamber, worked from ca 1743 ; the bust of the king who had the customary rights of the miners written down (1368), rock-salt sculpture (1968) by the sculptor Władysław Hapek.

62. The Nicholas Copernicus Chamber, worked before 1785, with the sculpture of the great Polish astronomer, rock-salt sculpture (1973) by the artist Władysław Hapek.

63. The Józef Piłsudski Chamber, worked in 1810--1830 rock-salt sculpture of the Marshal by the miner sculptor Stanisław Anioł, carved in 1997, when the chamber assumed its former name again.

64. The Kunegunda shaft bottom: here for the youngest visitors the miner Stefan Kozik carved in rock-salt (1962-1964) the figures of gnomes, who are believed to help the hard-working Wieliczka miners.

65. In 1790 the Wieliczka Mine was visited by Johann Wolfgang von Goethe. To commemorate his visit, a chamber with a salt lake was named the Weimar Chamber, and in 2001 the poet's figure carved in rock-salt by the miner sculptor Józef Piotr Kowalczyk was placed at the entrance.

66, 67. He, the Warden of the Wieliczka Mine, takes care of the safety of the miners and warns them of disasters; rock--salt sculptures (1968) by the miner sculptors Mieczysław Kluzek and Antoni Cholewa, in Poniatowski Traverse. Below: the Weimar Chamber; the rock-salt sculpture of the Warden by the miner sculptor Stanisław Anioł, which represented the Wieliczka Mine at the World EXPO in 2000 in Hanover. A block of rock-salt was placed on a pushcart, and world leaders and numerous visitors to the Polish pavilion 'carved' in it.

68. Salt crystals in the Wieliczka Mine. →

IN THE LAND
OF SALT CRYSTALS

69-71. The crystal Caves are in the block stratum of the Wieliczka Mine (at the depth of ca 80 m). They are unique in Miocene mineralogy in respect of the size and number of the sets of crystals, and are spectacular because of their beautiful halite crystals, the largest of them with edges 50 cm long.

72-75. The water which penetrates the mine is the most dangerous element, but it also adorns the mine, as it produces various forms of crystallised salt.

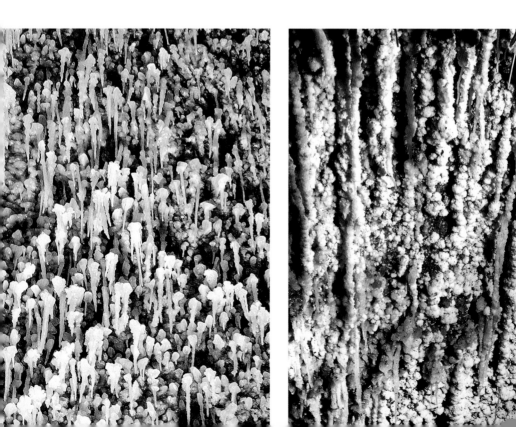

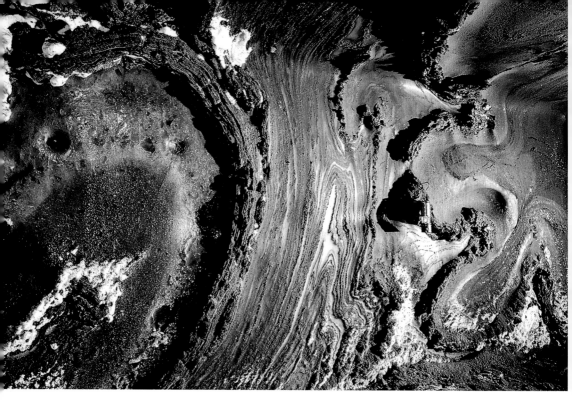

76, 77. Tectonic movements have produced the fascinating patterns of the Wieliczka salt deposit (above) and salt crystallisation has taken such exquisite forms as 'Kinga's Hair'.

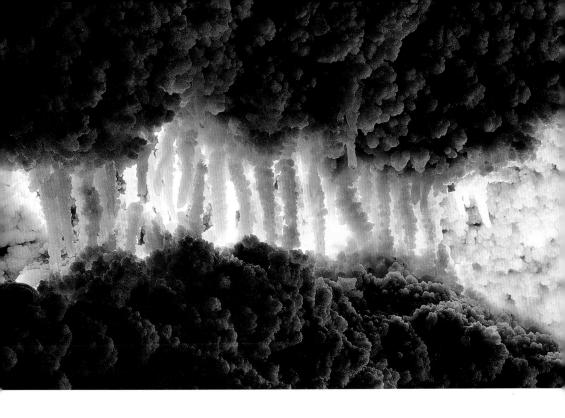

78, 79. Salt stalactites and stalagmites in the Wieliczka Mine soon merge and produce admirable stalagmites.

Published in cooperation with
THE 'WIELICZKA' SALT MINE, THE TOURIST ROUTE LTD.; www.kopalnia.pl

Photographs and computer processed photographs
© JANUSZ PODLECKI
e-mail: podlecki@kr.onet.pl

Texts
© STANISŁAW ANIOŁ
including opinions of Józef Piotrowicz,
Studies and Materials on the History of Salt Mines in Poland, vol. XXI,
Museum of Cracow Salt Mines, Wieliczka 2001

Mine plan
© MARIUSZ SZELEREWICZ

Graphic design
© JULIAN PRZEMYSKI

Translated into English by
JADWIGA PIĄTKOWSKA

Consultants
STANISŁAW ANIOŁ

Printed by
FINIDR, s.r.o., Český Těšin, Czech Republic

Fourth edition, 2012

ISBN 978-83-61928-10-2

WYDAWNICTWO „KARPATY" – ANDRZEJ ŁĄCZYŃSKI
30-074 Kraków, ul. Kazimierza Wielkiego 21; e-mail: krakow@wydawnictwokarpaty.pl
www.wydawnictwokarpaty.pl